Just Ducky Baby Afghans

TABLE OF CONTENTS

Leisure Arts • Maumelle Arkansas

GENERAL INSTRUCTIONS

ABBREVIATIONS

BP	Back Post
BPdc	Back Post double crochet(s)
BPtr	Back Post treble crochet(s)
ch(s)	chain(s)
dc	double crochet(s)
FP	Front Post
FPdc	Front Post double crochet(s)
FPtr	Front Post treble crochet(s)
hdc	half double crochet(s)
mm	millimeters
Rnd(s)	Round(s)
sc	single crochet(s)
sp(s)	space(s)
st(s)	stitch(es)
tr	treble crochet(s)
YO	yarn over

★ — work instructions following ★ as many **more** times as indicated in addition to the first time.

† to † — work all instructions from first † to second † **as many** times as specified.

( ) or **[ ]** — work enclosed instructions **as many** times as specified by the number immediately following **or** work all enclosed instructions in the stitch or space indicated **or** contains explanatory remarks.

colon (:) — the number(s) given after a colon at the end of a row or round denote(s) the number of stitches you should have on that row or round.

CROCHET TERMINOLOGY	
UNITED STATES	**INTERNATIONAL**
slip stitch (slip st)	= single crochet (sc)
single crochet (sc)	= double crochet (dc)
half double crochet (hdc)	= half treble crochet (htr)
double crochet (dc)	= treble crochet (tr)
treble crochet (tr)	= double treble crochet (dtr)
double treble crochet (dtr)	= triple treble crochet (ttr)
skip	= miss

ALUMINUM CROCHET HOOKS						
U.S.	E-4	F-5	G-6	H-8	I-9	J-10
Metric - mm	3.50	3.75	4.00	5.00	5.50	6.00

BACK LOOP ONLY

Work only in loop(s) indicated by arrow ***(Fig. 1)***.

Fig. 1

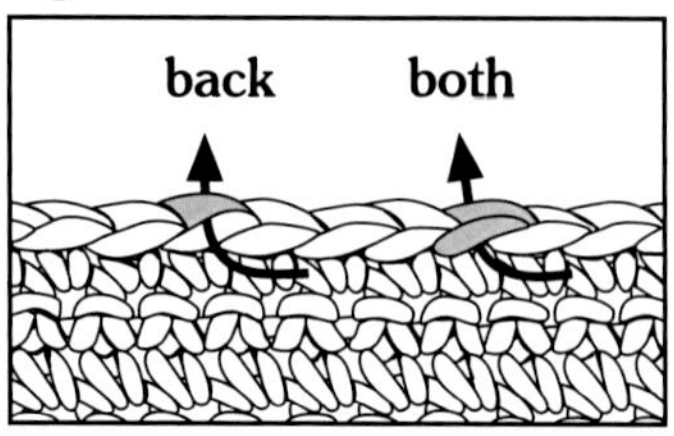

BACK RIDGE

Work only in loops indicated by arrows ***(Fig. 2)***.

Fig. 2

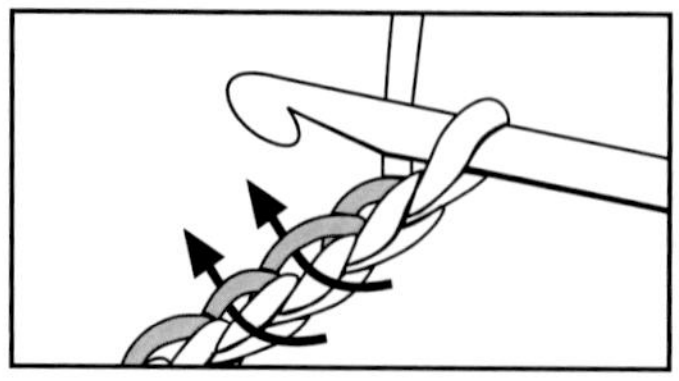

FREE LOOPS OF A CHAIN

When instructed to work in free loops of a chain, work in loop indicated by arrow ***(Fig. 3)***.

Fig. 3

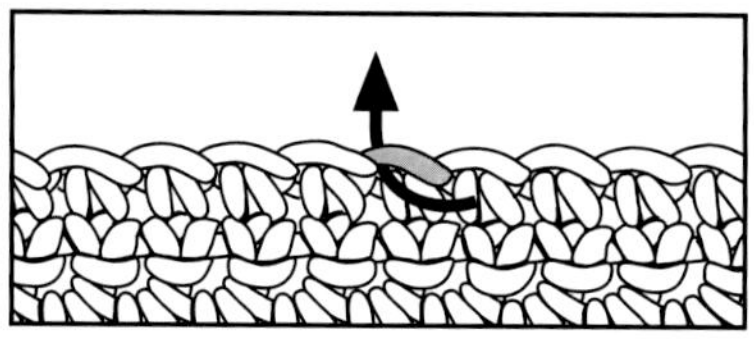

POST STITCH

Work around post of stitch indicated, inserting hook in direction of arrow ***(Fig. 4)***.

Fig. 4

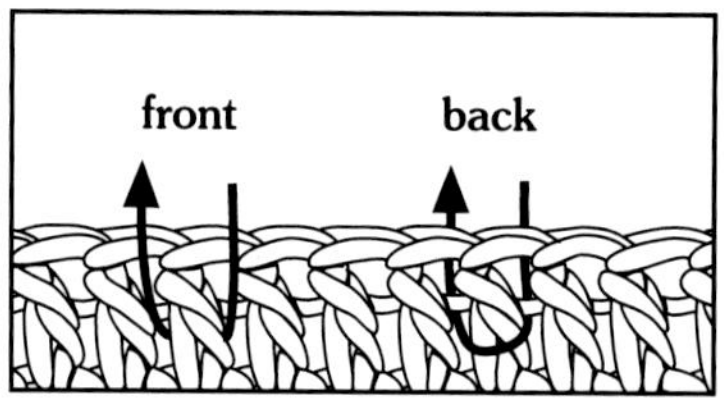

SATIN STITCH

Satin Stitch is a series of straight stitches worked side by side so they touch but do not overlap. Come up at odd numbers and go down at even numbers ***(Fig. 5)***.

Fig. 5

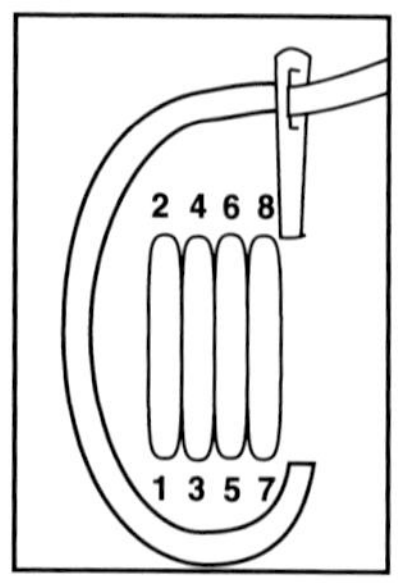

3

1. ROCK-A-BYE BABY

Shown on page 9.

Finished Size: 32½" x 44½"

MATERIALS

Sport Weight Yarn:
14 ounces, (400 grams, 1,490 yards)
Crochet hook, size G (4.00 mm) **or** size needed for gauge

GAUGE: In pattern, from point to point = 6½";
6 rows = 4"

Gauge Swatch: 13"w x 4"h
Ch 78 **loosely**.
Work same as Afghan for 6 rows.
Finish off.

STITCH GUIDE

TREBLE CROCHET ***(abbreviated tr)***
YO twice, insert hook in st indicated, YO and pull up a loop (4 loops on hook), (YO and draw through 2 loops on hook) 3 times.

CLUSTER (uses next 5 sts)
★ YO, insert hook in **next** st, YO and pull up a loop, YO and draw through 2 loops on hook; repeat from ★ 4 times **more**, YO and draw through all 6 loops on hook.

BEGINNING DECREASE (uses next 2 dc)
★ YO, insert hook in **next** dc, YO and pull up a loop, YO and draw through 2 loops on hook; repeat from ★ once **more**, YO and draw through all 3 loops on hook **(counts as one dc)**.

ENDING DECREASE (uses last 3 dc)
★ YO, insert hook in **next** dc, YO and pull up a loop, YO and draw through 2 loops on hook; repeat from ★ 2 times **more**, YO and draw through all 4 loops on hook **(counts as one dc)**.

FRONT POST TREBLE CROCHET ***(abbreviated FPtr)***
YO twice, insert hook from **front** to **back** around post of st indicated ***(Fig. 4, page 2)***, YO and pull up a loop (4 loops on hook), (YO and draw through 2 loops on hook) 3 times.

BACK POST TREBLE CROCHET ***(abbreviated BPtr)***
YO twice, insert hook from **back** to **front** around post of st indicated ***(Fig. 4, page 2)***, YO and pull up a loop (4 loops on hook), (YO and draw through 2 loops on hook) 3 times.

AFGHAN BODY

Ch 192 **loosely**.

Row 1 (Right side)**:** Dc in third ch from hook and in next 9 chs, ch 2, skip next 2 chs, dc in next 3 chs, ch 1, skip next 3 chs, (3 dc, ch 3, 3 dc) in next ch, ch 1, skip next 3 chs, dc in next 3 chs, ch 2, ★ skip next 2 chs, dc in next 8 chs, work Cluster, dc in next 8 chs, ch 2, skip next 2 chs, dc in next 3 chs, ch 1, skip next 3 chs, (3 dc, ch 3, 3 dc) in next ch, ch 1, skip next 3 chs, dc in next 3 chs, ch 2; repeat from ★ across to last 13 chs, skip next 2 chs, dc in next 9 chs, (YO, insert hook in **next** ch, YO and pull up a loop, YO and draw through 2 loops on hook) twice, YO and draw through all 3 loops on hook: 148 sts and 25 sps.

Note: Loop a short piece of yarn around any stitch to mark Row 1 as **right** side.

Row 2: Ch 2, turn; skip first st, work beginning decrease, dc in next 7 dc, 2 dc in next ch-2 sp, ch 2, skip next 2 dc, dc in next dc, working **behind** next ch-1, tr in center ch of next 3 skipped chs on beginning ch, dc in next dc, ch 1, (3 dc, ch 3, 3 dc) in next ch-3 sp, ★ † ch 1, skip next 2 dc, dc in next dc, working **behind** next ch-1, tr in center ch of next 3 skipped chs on beginning ch, dc in next dc, ch 2, 2 dc in next ch-2 sp †, dc in next 6 dc, work Cluster, dc in next 6 dc, 2 dc in next ch-2 sp, ch 2, skip next 2 dc, dc in next dc, working **behind** next ch-1, tr in center ch of next 3 skipped chs on beginning ch, dc in next dc, ch 1, (3 dc, ch 3, 3 dc) in next ch-3 sp; repeat from ★ 3 times **more**, then repeat from † to † once, dc in next 7 dc, work ending decrease.

Row 3: Ch 2, turn; skip first dc, work beginning decrease, dc in next 7 dc, 2 dc in next ch-2 sp, ch 2, skip next 2 sts, dc in next dc, working in **front** of next ch-1, work FPtr around first skipped dc one row **below**, dc in next dc, ch 1, (3 dc, ch 3, 3 dc) in next ch-3 sp, ★ † ch 1, skip next 2 dc, dc in next dc, working in **front** of next ch-1, work FPtr around second skipped dc one row **below**, dc in next dc, ch 2, 2 dc in next ch-2 sp †, dc in next 6 dc, work Cluster, dc in next 6 dc, 2 dc in next ch-2 sp, ch 2, skip next 2 sts, dc in next dc, working in **front** of next ch-1, work FPtr around first skipped dc one row **below**, dc in next dc, ch 1, (3 dc, ch 3, 3 dc) in next ch-3 sp; repeat from ★ 3 times **more**, then repeat from † to † once, dc in next 7 dc, work ending decrease.

Row 4: Ch 2, turn; skip first dc, work beginning decrease, dc in next 7 dc, 2 dc in next ch-2 sp, ch 2, skip next 2 sts, dc in next dc, working **behind** next ch-1, work BPtr around first skipped dc one row **below**, dc in next dc, ch 1, (3 dc, ch 3, 3 dc) in next ch-3 sp, ★ † ch 1, skip next 2 dc, dc in next dc, working **behind** next ch-1, work BPtr around second skipped dc one row **below**, dc in next dc, ch 2, 2 dc in next ch-2 sp †, dc in next 6 dc, work Cluster, dc in next 6 dc, 2 dc in next ch-2 sp, ch 2, skip next 2 sts, dc in next dc, working **behind** next ch-1, work BPtr around first skipped dc one row **below**, dc in next dc, ch 1, (3 dc, ch 3, 3 dc) in next ch-3 sp; repeat from ★ 3 times **more**, then repeat from † to † once, dc in next 7 dc, work ending decrease.

Rows 5-66: Repeat Rows 3 and 4, 31 times.

Row 67: Ch 1, turn; pull up a loop in first 2 dc, YO and draw through all 3 loops on hook, sc in next 8 dc, 2 sc in next ch-2 sp, sc in next 3 sts, working in **front** of next ch-1, work FPtr around first skipped dc one row **below**, sc in next 3 dc, 3 sc in next ch-3 sp, ★ † sc in next 3 dc, working in **front** of next ch-1, work FPtr around second skipped dc one row **below**, sc in next 3 sts, 2 sc in next ch-2 sp †, sc in next 7 dc, pull up a loop in next 3 sts, YO and draw through all 4 loops on hook, sc in next 7 dc, 2 sc in next ch-2 sp, sc in next 3 sts, working in **front** of next ch-1, work FPtr around first skipped dc one row **below**, sc in next 3 dc, 3 sc in next ch-3 sp; repeat from ★ 3 times **more**, then repeat from † to † once, sc in next 8 dc, pull up a loop in last 2 dc, YO and draw through all 3 loops on hook; finish off.

TRIM

With **right** side facing and working in free loops of beginning ch ***(Fig. 3, page 2)***, join yarn with slip st in first ch; ch 1, 2 sc in same ch, sc in next 17 chs, pull up a loop in next 3 chs, YO and draw through all 4 loops on hook, sc in next 17 chs, ★ 3 sc in next ch, sc in next 17 chs, pull up a loop in next 3 chs, YO and draw through all 4 loops on hook, sc in next 17 chs; repeat from ★ 3 times **more**, 2 sc in next ch; finish off.

---

2. PLAYTIME

Shown on pages 8-9.

Finished Size: 35" x 45½"

MATERIALS

Sport Weight Yarn:
- White - 11 ounces, (310 grams, 1,170 yards)
- Blue - 3 ounces, (90 grams, 320 yards)
- Pink - 3 ounces, (90 grams, 320 yards)

Crochet hook, size G (4.00 mm) **or** size needed for gauge

GAUGE: In pattern, from point to point = 7";
8 rows = 4"

Gauge Swatch: 14"w x 4"h
Ch 79 **loosely**.
Work same as Afghan for 8 rows.
Finish off.

STITCH GUIDE

SC DECREASE
Pull up a loop in next dc, pull up a loop in next ch-1 sp and in next dc, YO and draw through all 4 loops on hook.

DC DECREASE
YO, insert hook in same sp, YO and pull up a loop, YO and draw through 2 loops on hook, YO, insert hook in next ch-3 sp, YO and pull up a loop, YO and draw through 2 loops on hook, YO and draw through all 3 loops on hook.

ENDING DECREASE
YO, insert hook in next ch-3 sp, YO and pull up a loop, YO and draw through 2 loops on hook, YO, insert hook in last st, YO and pull up a loop, YO and draw through 2 loops on hook, YO and draw through all 3 loops on hook.

AFGHAN BODY

With Blue, ch 192 **loosely**.

Row 1 (Right side)**:** Dc in third ch from hook, ch 1, ★ † skip next 2 chs, (3 dc in next ch, ch 1, skip next 2 chs) 5 times, (3 dc, ch 3, 3 dc) in next ch, ch 1, skip next 2 chs, (3 dc in next ch, ch 1, skip next 2 chs) 5 times †, (YO, insert hook in **next** ch, YO and pull up a loop, YO and draw through 2 loops on hook) 3 times, YO and draw through all 4 loops on hook, ch 1; repeat from ★ 3 times **more**, then repeat from † to † once, (YO, insert hook in **next** ch, YO and pull up a loop, YO and draw through 2 loops on hook) twice, YO and draw through all 3 loops on hook; finish off: 186 sts and 65 sps.

Note: Loop a short piece of yarn around any stitch to mark Row 1 as **right** side.

Row 2: With **right** side facing, join White with slip st in first dc; ch 1, pull up a loop in same st, pull up a loop in next ch-1 sp and in next dc, YO and draw through all 4 loops on hook, ch 3, skip next dc, (sc decrease, ch 3, skip next dc) 5 times, ★ † pull up a loop in next dc and in next ch-3 sp, YO and draw through all 3 loops on hook, ch 3, pull up a loop in same sp and in next dc, YO and draw through all 3 loops on hook †, ch 3, skip next dc, (sc decrease, ch 3, skip next dc) 5 times, pull up a loop in next dc, pull up a loop in next 2 ch-1 sps and in next dc, YO and draw through all 5 loops on hook, ch 3, skip next dc, (sc decrease, ch 3, skip next dc) 5 times; repeat from ★ 3 times **more**, then repeat from † to † once, (ch 3, skip next dc, sc decrease) across: 65 ch-3 sps.

Row 3: Ch 2, turn; dc in next ch-3 sp, ch 1, (3 dc in next ch-3 sp, ch 1) 5 times, (3 dc, ch 3, 3 dc) in next ch-3 sp, ch 1, (3 dc in next ch-3 sp, ch 1) 5 times, ★ dc in next ch-3 sp, dc decrease, dc in same sp, ch 1, (3 dc in next ch-3 sp, ch 1) 5 times, (3 dc, ch 3, 3 dc) in next ch-3 sp, ch 1, (3 dc in next ch-3 sp, ch 1) 5 times; repeat from ★ 3 times **more**, work ending decrease; do **not** finish off: 194 sts and 65 sps.

Continued on page 6.

Row 4: Ch 1, turn; pull up a loop in first st, pull up a loop in next ch-1 sp and in next dc, YO and draw through all 4 loops on hook, ch 3, skip next dc, (sc decrease, ch 3, skip next dc) 5 times, ★ † pull up a loop in next dc and in next ch-3 sp, YO and draw through all 3 loops on hook, ch 3, pull up a loop in same sp and in next dc, YO and draw through all 3 loops on hook †, ch 3, skip next dc, (sc decrease, ch 3, skip next dc) 5 times, pull up a loop in next dc, pull up a loop in next 2 ch-1 sps and in next dc, YO and draw through all 5 loops on hook, ch 3, skip next dc, (sc decrease, ch 3, skip next dc) 5 times; repeat from ★ 3 times **more**, then repeat from † to † once, (ch 3, skip next dc, sc decrease) across; finish off: 65 ch-3 sps.

Row 5: With **right** side facing, join Pink with slip st in first st; ch 2, dc in next ch-3 sp, ch 1, (3 dc in next ch-3 sp, ch 1) 5 times, (3 dc, ch 3, 3 dc) in next ch-3 sp, ch 1, (3 dc in next ch-3 sp, ch 1) 5 times, ★ dc in next ch-3 sp, dc decrease, dc in same sp, ch 1, (3 dc in next ch-3 sp, ch 1) 5 times, (3 dc, ch 3, 3 dc) in next ch-3 sp, ch 1, (3 dc in next ch-3 sp, ch 1) 5 times; repeat from ★ 3 times **more**, work ending decrease; finish off: 194 sts and 65 sps.

Rows 6-8: Repeat Rows 2-4.

Row 9: With Blue, repeat Row 5.

Rows 10-90: Repeat Rows 2-9, 10 times; then repeat Row 2 once **more**.

Finish off.

TRIM

With **right** side facing and working in free loops of beginning ch ***(Fig. 3, page 2)***, join White with slip st in first ch; ch 1, pull up a loop in same ch and in next ch, YO and draw through all 3 loops on hook, ch 3, ★ † (pull up a loop in next 2 chs, YO and draw through all 3 loops on hook, ch 3, skip next ch) 5 times, pull up a loop in next 2 chs, skip next ch, pull up a loop in next 2 chs, YO and draw through all 5 loops on hook, ch 3, (skip next ch, pull up a loop in next 2 chs, YO and draw through all 3 loops on hook, ch 3) 5 times, pull up a loop in next 2 chs, YO and draw through all 3 loops on hook †, ch 3, pull up a loop in same ch and in next ch, YO and draw through all 3 loops on hook, ch 3; repeat from ★ 3 times **more**, then repeat from † to † once; finish off.

3. CUDDLESOFT

Shown on page 3.

Finished Size: 36½" x 46½"

MATERIALS

Sport Weight Yarn:

Solid Color Afghan

19½ ounces, (550 grams, 2,070 yards)

Striped Afghan

Blue - 7¾ ounces, (220 grams, 825 yards)
Yellow - 7 ounces, (200 grams, 745 yards)
White - 4¾ ounces, (135 grams, 505 yards)

Crochet hook, size H (5.00 mm) **or** size needed for gauge

GAUGE: In pattern, from point to point and 8 rows = 4½"

Gauge Swatch: 9"w x 4½"h
With Blue, ch 44 **loosely**.
Work same as Afghan for 8 rows.
Finish off.

STITCH GUIDE

BACK POST DOUBLE CROCHET
(abbreviated BPdc)
YO, insert hook from **back** to **front** around post of st indicated ***(Fig. 4, page 2)***, YO and pull up a loop (3 loops on hook), (YO and draw through 2 loops on hook) twice. Skip st in front of BPdc.

FRONT POST DOUBLE CROCHET
(abbreviated FPdc)
YO, insert hook from **front** to **back** around post of st indicated ***(Fig. 4, page 2)***, YO and pull up a loop (3 loops on hook), (YO and draw through 2 loops on hook) twice. Skip st behind FPdc.

BACK POST CLUSTER
(abbreviated BP Cluster) (uses next 2 sts)
★ YO, insert hook from **back** to **front** around post of **next** st ***(Fig. 4, page 2)***, YO and pull up a loop, (YO and draw through 2 loops on hook); repeat from ★ once **more**, YO and draw though all 3 loops on hook.

FRONT POST CLUSTER
(abbreviated FP Cluster) (uses next 2 sts)
★ YO, insert hook from **front** to **back** around post of **next** st ***(Fig. 4, page 2)***, YO and pull up a loop, (YO and draw through 2 loops on hook); repeat from ★ once **more**, YO and draw though all 3 loops on hook.

SOLID COLOR AFGHAN

Ch 164 **loosely**.

Row 1 (Right side)**:** 2 Dc in fourth ch from hook and in next ch **(3 skipped chs count as first dc)**, (ch 1, skip next ch, dc in next ch) 3 times, skip next ch, dc in next 2 chs, (skip next ch, dc in next ch, ch 1) 3 times, ★ skip next ch, 2 dc in each of next 4 chs, (ch 1, skip next ch, dc in next ch) 3 times, skip next ch, dc in next 2 chs, (skip next ch, dc in next ch, ch 1) 3 times; repeat from ★ across to last 4 chs, skip next ch, 2 dc in each of next 2 chs, dc in last ch: 130 dc and 48 ch-1 sps.

Note: Loop a short piece of yarn around any stitch to mark Row 1 as **right** side.

Row 2: Ch 3 **(counts as first dc, now and throughout)**, turn; 2 dc in each of next 2 dc, ch 1, skip next dc, (work BPdc around next st, ch 1) 3 times, work BP Cluster twice, ch 1, (work BPdc around next st, ch 1) 3 times, ★ skip next dc, 2 dc in each of next 4 dc, ch 1, skip next dc, (work BPdc around next st, ch 1) 3 times, work BP Cluster twice, ch 1, (work BPdc around next st, ch 1) 3 times; repeat from ★ across to last 4 dc, skip next dc, 2 dc in each of next 2 dc, dc in last dc.

Row 3: Ch 3, turn; 2 dc in each of next 2 dc, ch 1, skip next dc, (work FPdc around next st, ch 1) 3 times, work FP Cluster twice, ch 1, (work FPdc around next st, ch 1) 3 times, ★ skip next dc, 2 dc in each of next 4 dc, ch 1, skip next dc, (work FPdc around next st, ch 1) 3 times, work FP Cluster twice, ch 1, (work FPdc around next st, ch 1) 3 times; repeat from ★ across to last 4 dc, skip next dc, 2 dc in each of next 2 dc, dc in last dc.

Repeat Rows 2 and 3, until Afghan measures approximately 46" from beginning ch, ending by working Row 3.

Finish off.

EDGING

With **right** side facing, join yarn with slip st in first dc on last row; ch 1, 3 sc in same st, sc in next 4 dc, (sc in next ch-1 sp and in next FPdc) 3 times, pull up a loop in next ch-1 sp, pull up a loop in next 2 sts and in next ch-1 sp, YO and draw through all 5 loops on hook, (sc in next FPdc and in next ch-1 sp) 3 times, ★ sc in next 8 dc, (sc in next ch-1 sp and in next FPdc) 3 times, pull up a loop in next ch-1 sp, pull up a loop in next 2 sts and in next ch-1 sp, YO and draw through all 5 loops on hook, (sc in next FPdc and in next ch-1 sp) 3 times; repeat from ★ across to last 5 dc, sc in next 4 dc, 3 sc in last dc; sc evenly across end of rows; working in free loops of beginning ch ***(Fig. 3, page 2)***, 3 sc in first ch, sc in each ch across to ch at base of last dc, 3 sc in ch at base of last dc; sc evenly across end of rows; join with slip st to first sc, finish off.

STRIPED AFGHAN

With Blue, ch 164 **loosely**.

Row 1 (Right side)**:** 2 Dc in fourth ch from hook and in next ch **(3 skipped chs count as first dc)**, (ch 1, skip next ch, dc in next ch) 3 times, skip next ch, dc in next 2 chs, (skip next ch, dc in next ch, ch 1) 3 times, ★ skip next ch, 2 dc in each of next 4 chs, (ch 1, skip next ch, dc in next ch) 3 times, skip next ch, dc in next 2 chs, (skip next ch, dc in next ch, ch 1) 3 times; repeat from ★ across to last 4 chs, skip next ch, 2 dc in each of next 2 chs, dc in last ch: 130 dc and 48 ch-1 sps.

Note: Loop a short piece of yarn around any stitch to mark Row 1 as **right** side.

Row 2: Ch 3 **(counts as first dc, now and throughout)**, turn; 2 dc in each of next 2 dc, ch 1, skip next dc, (work BPdc around next st, ch 1) 3 times, work BP Cluster twice, ch 1, (work BPdc around next st, ch 1) 3 times, ★ skip next dc, 2 dc in each of next 4 dc, ch 1, skip next dc, (work BPdc around next st, ch 1) 3 times, work BP Cluster twice, ch 1, (work BPdc around next st, ch 1) 3 times; repeat from ★ across to last 4 dc, skip next dc, 2 dc in each of next 2 dc, dc in last dc.

Row 3: Ch 3, turn; 2 dc in each of next 2 dc, ch 1, skip next dc, (work FPdc around next st, ch 1) 3 times, work FP Cluster twice, ch 1, (work FPdc around next st, ch 1) 3 times, ★ skip next dc, 2 dc in each of next 4 dc, ch 1, skip next dc, (work FPdc around next st, ch 1) 3 times, work FP Cluster twice, ch 1, (work FPdc around next st, ch 1) 3 times; repeat from ★ across to last 4 dc, skip next dc, 2 dc in each of next 2 dc, dc in last dc; finish off.

Row 4: With **wrong** side facing, join White with slip st in first dc; ch 3, 2 dc in each of next 2 dc, ch 1, skip next dc, (work BPdc around next st, ch 1) 3 times, work BP Cluster twice, ch 1, (work BPdc around next st, ch 1) 3 times, ★ skip next dc, 2 dc in each of next 4 dc, ch 1, skip next dc, (work BPdc around next st, ch 1) 3 times, work BP Cluster twice, ch 1, (work BPdc around next st, ch 1) 3 times; repeat from ★ across to last 4 dc, skip next dc, 2 dc in each of next 2 dc, dc in last dc; finish off.

Row 5: With **right** side facing, join Yellow with slip st in first dc; ch 3, 2 dc in each of next 2 dc, ch 1, skip next dc, (work FPdc around next st, ch 1) 3 times, work FP Cluster twice, ch 1, (work FPdc around next st, ch 1) 3 times, ★ skip next dc, 2 dc in each of next 4 dc, ch 1, skip next dc, (work FPdc around next st, ch 1) 3 times, work FP Cluster twice, ch 1, (work FPdc around next st, ch 1) 3 times; repeat from ★ across to last 4 dc, skip next dc, 2 dc in each of next 2 dc, dc in last dc.

Rows 6-8: Repeat Rows 2-4.

Row 9: With Blue, Repeat Row 5.

Rows 10-83: Repeat Rows 2-9, 9 times; then repeat Rows 2 and 3 once **more**.

EDGING

With Blue, work same as Solid Color Afghan.

6

2

1

4. HAPPY TIMES

Shown on Front Cover

Finished Size: 37½" x 49"

MATERIALS

Sport Weight Yarn:
- White - 10½ ounces, (300 grams, 1,115 yards)
- Blue - 5 ounces, (140 grams, 530 yards)
- Yellow - 4½ ounces, (130 grams, 480 yards)

Crochet hook, size G (4.00 mm) **or** size needed for gauge

GAUGE: In pattern, from point to point = 7½";
8 rows = 4¾"

Gauge Swatch: 15"w x 4¾"h
Ch 79 **loosely**.
Work same as Afghan for 8 rows.
Finish off.

STITCH GUIDE

TREBLE CROCHET ***(abbreviated tr)***
YO twice, insert hook in sp indicated, YO and pull up a loop (4 loops on hook), (YO and draw through 2 loops on hook) 3 times.

CROSS STITCH ***(abbreviated Cross St)***
Skip next 3 dc, tr in sp **before** next st, ch 2, working **behind** tr just made, tr in same sp as first leg of last Cross St made.

CLUSTER
YO, insert hook in next ch-2 sp, YO and pull up a loop, YO and draw through 2 loops on hook, skip next tr, ★ YO, insert hook in **next** tr, YO and pull up a loop, YO and draw through 2 loops on hook; repeat from ★ once **more**, YO, insert hook in next ch-2 sp, YO and pull up a loop, YO and draw through 2 loops on hook, YO and draw through all 5 loops on hook.

AFGHAN BODY

With Blue, ch 196 **loosely**.

Row 1 (Wrong side)**:** Dc in third ch from hook, ★ † skip next 2 chs, (3 dc in next ch, skip next 2 chs) 5 times, (3 dc, ch 1, 3 dc) in next ch, skip next 2 chs, (3 dc in next ch, skip next 2 chs) 5 times †, (YO, insert hook in **next** ch, YO and pull up a loop, YO and draw through 2 loops on hook) 4 times, YO and draw through all 5 loops on hook **(Cluster made)**; repeat from ★ 3 times **more**, then repeat from † to † once, (YO, insert hook in **next** ch, YO and pull up a loop, YO and draw through 2 loops on hook) twice, YO and draw through all 3 loops on hook; finish off: 60 3-dc groups and 5 ch-1 sps.

Note: Loop a short piece of yarn around the **back** of any stitch to mark **right** side.

Row 2: With **right** side facing, join White with slip st in first st; ch 2, skip next 3 dc, tr in sp **before** next dc, ch 2, working **behind** tr just made, tr in sp **before** 3 skipped dc **(Cross St made)**, work 4 Cross Sts, ★ † skip next 3 dc, tr in next ch-1 sp, ch 2, working **behind** tr just made, tr in same sp as first leg of last Cross St made **(Cross St made)**, (tr, ch 2, tr) in same ch-1 sp †, work 6 Cross Sts, skip next Cluster, tr in sp **before** next dc, working **behind** tr just made, tr in same sp as first leg of last Cross St made **(Cross St made)**, work 5 Cross Sts; repeat from ★ 3 times **more**, then repeat from † to † once, work 5 Cross Sts, skip next 3 dc, tr in sp **before** next dc, ch 2, YO twice, working **behind** tr just made, insert hook in same sp as first leg of last Cross St made, YO and pull up a loop (4 loops on hook), (YO and draw through 2 loops on hook) twice, YO, insert hook in last dc, YO and pull up a loop, YO and draw through 2 loops on hook, YO and draw through all 3 loops on hook; finish off: 65 ch-2 sps.

Row 3: With **wrong** side facing, join Yellow with slip st in first st; ch 2, dc in next ch-2 sp, 3 dc in each of next 5 ch-2 sps, (3 dc, ch 1, 3 dc) in next ch-2 sp, 3 dc in each of next 5 ch-2 sps, ★ work Cluster, 3 dc in each of next 5 ch-2 sps, (3 dc, ch 1, 3 dc) in next ch-2 sp, 3 dc in each of next 5 ch-2 sps; repeat from ★ 3 times **more**, YO, insert hook in next ch-2 sp, YO and pull up a loop, YO and draw through 2 loops on hook, YO, insert hook in last tr, YO and pull up a loop, YO and draw through 2 loops on hook, YO and draw through all 3 loops on hook; finish off: 60 3-dc groups and 5 ch-1 sps.

Row 4: Repeat Row 2.

Row 5: With Blue, repeat Row 3.

Rows 6-81: Repeat Rows 2-5, 19 times; at end of Row 81, do **not** finish off.

Row 82: Ch 1, turn; skip first st, sc in next 18 dc, sc in next ch-1 sp and in next 17 dc, ★ pull up a loop in next 3 sts, YO and draw through all 4 loops on hook, sc in next 17 dc, sc in next ch-1 sp and in next 17 dc; repeat from ★ 3 times **more**, pull up a loop in last 2 dc, YO and draw all through 3 loops on hook; finish off.

TRIM

With **right** side facing and working in sps and in free loops of beginning ch ***(Fig. 3, page 2)***, join Blue with slip st in ch at base of first dc; ch 1, 2 sc in same ch, ★ † (2 sc in next ch-2 sp, sc in next ch) 5 times, sc in next ch-2 sp, pull up a loop in same sp, pull up a loop in next ch and in next ch-2 sp, YO and draw through all 4 loops on hook, sc in same sp, (sc in next ch, 2 sc in next ch-2 sp) 5 times, sc in next 2 chs †, sc in sp **before** next ch, sc in next 2 chs; repeat from ★ 3 times **more**, then repeat from † to † once; finish off.

5. LULLABY

White afghan shown on Back Cover

Finished Size: $37\frac{1}{2}$" x 47"

MATERIALS

Sport Weight Yarn:
18 ounces, (510 grams, 1,915 yards)
Crochet hook, size H (5.00 mm) **or** size needed for gauge

GAUGE: In pattern, from point to point = $6\frac{1}{4}$";
5 rows = $2\frac{1}{2}$"

Gauge Swatch: $12\frac{1}{2}$"w x $2\frac{1}{2}$"h
Ch 64 **loosely**.
Work same as Afghan for 5 rows.
Finish off.

STITCH GUIDE

2-DC CLUSTER (uses one st or sp)
YO, insert hook in st or sp indicated, YO and pull up a loop, YO and draw through 2 loops on hook, YO, insert hook in same st or sp, YO and pull up a loop, YO and draw through 2 loops on hook, YO and draw through all 3 loops on hook.

5-DC CLUSTER (uses next 5 sts)
★ YO, insert hook in **next** st **or** sp, YO and pull up a loop, YO and draw through 2 loops on hook; repeat from ★ 4 times **more**, YO and draw through all 6 loops on hook.

SC DECREASE
Pull up a loop in next 3 sts, YO and draw through all 4 loops on hook **(counts as one sc)**.

DC DECREASE (uses next 2 sts)
★ YO, insert hook in **next** st, YO and pull up a loop, YO and draw through 2 loops on hook; repeat from ★ once **more**, YO and draw through all 3 loops on hook.

SHELL (uses one sc)
Work 2-dc Cluster in sc indicated, (ch 1, work 2-dc Cluster in same st) twice.

AFGHAN BODY

Ch 192 **loosely**, place marker in second ch from hook for stitch placement.

Row 1: Dc in third ch from hook and in next 13 chs, 5 dc in next ch, dc in next 13 chs, ★ work 5-dc Cluster, dc in next 13 chs, 5 dc in next ch, dc in next 13 chs; repeat from ★ across to last 2 chs, dc decrease: 193 sts.

Row 2 (Right side)**:** Ch 2, turn; skip first st, dc in next 15 dc, 5 dc in next dc, ★ dc in next 13 dc, work 5-dc Cluster, dc in next 13 dc, 5 dc in next dc; repeat from ★ 4 times **more**, dc in next 14 dc, dc decrease: 195 sts.

Note: Loop a short piece of yarn around any stitch to mark Row 2 as **right** side.

Row 3: Ch 1, turn; skip first st, sc in next dc, ch 3, (skip next 2 dc, sc in next dc, ch 3) 5 times, skip next dc, sc in next dc, ★ (ch 3, skip next 2 dc, sc in next dc) 4 times, ch 1, skip next dc, sc decrease, ch 1, skip next dc, sc in next dc, ch 3, (skip next 2 dc, sc in next dc, ch 3) 4 times, skip next dc, sc in next dc; repeat from ★ 4 times **more**, ch 3, skip next 2 dc, (sc in next dc, ch 3, skip next 2 dc) 4 times, pull up a loop in last 2 dc, YO and draw through all 3 loops on hook: 66 sps.

Row 4: Ch 1, turn; sc in center ch of first ch-3, work Shell in next sc, sc in next ch-3 sp, (ch 1, sc in next ch-3 sp, work Shell in next sc, sc in next ch-3 sp) twice, ★ (work Shell in next sc, sc in next ch-3 sp, ch 1, sc in next ch-3 sp) twice, work 2-dc Cluster in next ch-1 sp, ch 1, work 2-dc Cluster in next sc, ch 1, work 2-dc Cluster in next ch-1 sp, sc in next ch-3 sp, (ch 1, sc in next ch-3 sp, work Shell in next sc, sc in next ch-3 sp) twice; repeat from ★ 4 times **more**, work Shell in next sc, (sc in next ch-3 sp, ch 1, sc in next ch-3 sp, work Shell in next sc) twice, sc in center ch of last ch-3: 86 ch-1 sps.

Row 5: Ch 2, turn; sc in first ch-1 sp, ch 1, sc in next ch-1 sp, ch 2, (dc in next ch-1 sp, ch 2, sc in next ch-1 sp, ch 1, sc in next ch-1 sp, ch 2) twice, (dc, ch 2, dc) in next sc, ★ (ch 2, sc in next ch-1 sp, ch 1, sc in next ch-1 sp, ch 2, dc in next ch-1 sp) twice, ch 1, pull up a loop in next 2 ch-1 sps, YO and draw through all 3 loops on hook, ch 1, (dc in next ch-1 sp, ch 2, sc in next ch-1 sp, ch 1, sc in next ch-1 sp, ch 2) twice, (dc, ch 2, dc) in next sc; repeat from ★ 4 times **more**, ch 2, sc in next ch-1 sp, ch 1, sc in next ch-1 sp, (ch 2, dc in next ch-1 sp, ch 2, sc in next ch-1 sp, ch 1, sc in next ch-1 sp) twice; do **not** finish off: 92 sps.

Continued on page 12.

Row 6: Ch 2, turn; skip first sc, dc in next sc, 2 dc in each of next 2 ch-2 sps, dc in next ch-1 sp, 2 dc in each of next 4 sps, 5 dc in next ch-2 sp, ★ 2 dc in each of next 3 sps, dc in next dc, 2 dc in each of next 3 sps, work 5-dc Cluster, 2 dc in each of next 3 sps, dc in next dc, 2 dc in each of next 3 sps, 5 dc in next ch-2 sp; repeat from ★ 4 times **more**, 2 dc in each of next 4 sps, dc in next ch-1 sp, 2 dc in each of next 2 ch-2 sps, (YO, insert hook in **next** sc, YO and pull up a loop, YO and draw through 2 loops on hook) twice, YO and draw through all 3 loops on hook: 193 sts.

Row 7: Ch 2, turn; skip first st, dc in next 15 dc, 5 dc in next dc, ★ dc in next 13 dc, work 5-dc Cluster, dc in next 13 dc, 5 dc in next dc; repeat from ★ 4 times **more**, dc in next 14 dc, dc decrease: 195 sts.

Rows 8-92: Repeat Rows 3-7, 17 times; at end of Row 92, do **not** finish off.

EDGING

Ch 1, do **not** turn; 3 sc in top of last st on Row 92; † working in end of rows, skip first row, sc in next row, ch 3, skip next row, (sc in next row, ch 3) across to last 5 rows, skip next row, (sc in next row, ch 3, skip next row) twice †; working in free loops of beginning ch ***(Fig. 3, page 2)***, 5 sc in marked ch, (ch 3, skip next 2 chs, sc in next ch) 4 times, ch 2, skip next ch, sc decrease, ch 2, skip next ch, sc in next ch, ch 3, ★ (skip next 2 chs, sc in next ch, ch 3) 4 times, skip next ch, sc in next ch, (ch 3, skip next 2 chs, sc in next ch) 4 times, ch 2, skip next ch, sc decrease, ch 2, skip next ch, sc in next ch, ch 3; repeat from ★ 4 times **more**, skip next 2 chs, (sc in next ch, ch 3, skip next 2 chs) 3 times, 5 sc in next ch; repeat from † to † once; working in sts on Row 92, 3 sc in first dc, sc in next dc, ch 3, (skip next 2 dc, sc in next dc, ch 3) 5 times, skip next dc, sc in next dc, [(ch 3, skip next 2 dc, sc in next dc) 4 times, ch 2, skip next dc, sc decrease, ch 2, skip next dc, sc in next dc, ch 3, (skip next 2 dc, sc in next dc, ch 3) 4 times, skip next dc, sc in next dc] 5 times, (ch 3, skip next 2 dc, sc in next dc) 5 times; join with slip st to first sc, finish off.

6. SWEET DREAMS

Shown on page 8.

Finished Size: 34½" x 43½"

MATERIALS

Sport Weight Yarn:
- White - 9 ounces, (260 grams, 955 yards)
- Blue - 4½ ounces, (130 grams, 480 yards)
- Green - 4½ ounces, (130 grams, 480 yards)

Crochet hook, size G (4.00 mm) **or** size needed for gauge

GAUGE: In pattern, from point to point = 5¾"; 8 rows = 4"

Gauge Swatch: 11½"w x 4"h
Ch 56 **loosely**.
Work same as Afghan for 8 rows.
Finish off.

STITCH GUIDE

2-DC DECREASE (uses next 2 sts)
★ YO, insert hook in **next** st, YO and pull up a loop, YO and draw through 2 loops on hook; repeat from ★ once **more**, YO and draw through all 3 loops on hook **(counts as one dc)**.

3-DC DECREASE (uses next 3 sts)
★ YO, insert hook in **next** st, YO and pull up a loop, YO and draw through 2 loops on hook; repeat from ★ 2 times **more**, YO and draw through all 4 loops on hook **(counts as one dc)**.

FRONT POST DECREASE
(abbreviated FP decrease) (uses next 2 sts)
★ YO, insert hook from **front** to **back** around post of **next** st ***(Fig. 4, page 2)***, YO and pull up a loop, YO and draw through 2 loops on hook; repeat from ★ once **more**, YO and draw through all 3 loops on hook.

FRONT POST DOUBLE CROCHET
(abbreviated FPdc)
YO, insert hook from **front** to **back** around post of st indicated ***(Fig. 4, page 2)***, YO and pull up a loop (3 loops on hook), (YO and draw through 2 loops on hook) twice.

FRONT POST CLUSTER
(abbreviated FP Cluster) (uses next 3 sts)
★ YO, insert hook from **front** to **back** around post of **next** st ***(Fig. 4, page 2)***, YO and pull up a loop, YO and draw through 2 loops on hook; repeat from ★ 2 times **more**, YO and draw through all 4 loops on hook.

POPCORN
3 Dc in st indicated, drop loop from hook, insert hook in first dc of 3-dc group, hook dropped loop and draw through.

AFGHAN

With White, ch 168 **loosely**.

Row 1 (Right side)**:** Working in back ridges of beginning ch ***(Fig. 2, page 2)***, YO, insert hook in third ch from hook, YO and pull up a loop, YO and draw through 2 loops on hook, YO, insert hook in next ch, YO and pull up a loop, YO and draw through 2 loops on hook, YO and draw though all 3 loops on hook, dc in next 9 chs, 2 dc in next ch, 3 dc in next ch, 2 dc in next ch, dc in next 9 chs, ★ work 2-dc decrease, work 3-dc decrease, work 2-dc decrease, dc in next 9 chs, 2 dc in next ch, 3 dc in next ch, 2 dc in next ch, dc in next 9 chs; repeat from ★ across to last 3 chs, work 3-dc decrease: 167 sts.

Note: Loop a short piece of yarn around any stitch to mark Row 1 as **right** side.

Rows 2 and 3: Ch 2, turn; skip first st, work 2-dc decrease, dc in next 9 dc, 2 dc in next dc, 3 dc in next dc, 2 dc in next dc, dc in next 9 dc, ★ work 2-dc decrease, work 3-dc decrease, work 2-dc decrease, dc in next 9 dc, 2 dc in next dc, 3 dc in next dc, 2 dc in next dc, dc in next 9 dc; repeat from ★ across to last 3 sts, work 3-dc decrease.

Finish off.

Row 4: With **wrong** side facing, join Blue with slip st in first dc; ch 2, work FP decrease, work FPdc around each of next 9 dc, work 2 FPdc around next dc, work 3 FPdc around next dc, work 2 FPdc around next dc, work FPdc around each of next 9 dc, ★ work FP decrease, work FP Cluster, work FP decrease, work FPdc around each of next 9 dc, work 2 FPdc around next dc, work 3 FPdc around next dc, work 2 FPdc around next dc, work FPdc around each of next 9 dc; repeat from ★ across to last 3 sts, work FP Cluster.

Row 5: Ch 1, turn; sc in first st, (work Popcorn in next st, sc in next st) across: 84 sc and 83 Popcorns.

Row 6: Ch 1, turn; skip first sc, (YO, insert hook in **next** st, YO and pull up a loop) twice, YO and draw through all 5 loops on hook, hdc in next 9 sts, 2 hdc in next sc, 3 hdc in next Popcorn, 2 hdc in next sc, hdc in next 9 sts, ★ (YO, insert hook in **next** st, YO and pull up a loop) twice, YO and draw through all 5 loops on hook, (YO, insert hook in **next** st, YO and pull up a loop) 3 times, YO and draw through all 7 loops on hook, (YO, insert hook in **next** st, YO and pull up a loop) twice, YO and draw through all 5 loops on hook, hdc in next 9 sts, 2 hdc in next sc, 3 hdc in next Popcorn, 2 hdc in next sc, hdc in next 9 sts; repeat from ★ across to last 3 sts, (YO, insert hook in **next** st, YO and pull up a loop) 3 times, YO and draw through all 7 loops on hook; finish off: 167 sts.

Row 7: With **right** side facing, join White with slip st in first st; ch 1, sc in same st and in each st across.

Row 8: Ch 2, turn; work FP decrease, work FPdc around each of next 9 sc, work 2 FPdc around next sc, work 3 FPdc around next sc, work 2 FPdc around next sc, work FPdc around each of next 9 sc, ★ work FP decrease, work FP Cluster, work FP decrease, work FPdc around each of next 9 sc, work 2 FPdc around next sc, work 3 FPdc around next sc, work 2 FPdc around next sc, work FPdc around each of next 9 sc; repeat from ★ across to last 3 sc, work FP Cluster.

Rows 9 and 10: Repeat Rows 2 and 3.

Finish off.

Row 11: With Green, repeat Row 4.

Rows 12-17: Repeat Rows 5-10.

Finish off.

Rows 18-87: Repeat Rows 4-17, 5 times; at end of Row 87, do **not** finish off.

Row 88: Turn; slip st in each st across; finish off.

7. TICKLED PINK

Pink afghan shown on Back Cover

Finished Size: 35" x $45^1/_2$"

MATERIALS

Sport Weight Yarn:
Pink - 13 ounces, (370 grams, 1,380 yards)
White - 6 ounces, (170 grams, 640 yards)
Crochet hook, size G (4.00 mm) **or** size needed for gauge

GAUGE: In pattern, from point to point = 5";
10 rows = $4^1/_2$"

Gauge Swatch: 10"w x $4^1/_2$"h
Ch 56 **loosely**.
Work same as Afghan for 10 rows.
Finish off.

STITCH GUIDE

DECREASE (uses next 3 dc)
★ YO, insert hook in **next** dc, YO and pull up a loop, YO and draw through 2 loops on hook; repeat from ★ 2 times **more**, YO and draw through all 4 loops on hook **(counts as one dc)**.

DOUBLE DECREASE
YO, insert hook in next st, YO and pull up a loop, YO and draw through 2 loops on hook, ★ YO, skip **next** st or sp, insert hook in **next** st, YO and pull up a loop, YO and draw through 2 loops on hook; repeat from ★ once **more**, YO and draw through all 4 loops on hook **(counts as one dc)**.

ENDING DECREASE (uses last 2 sts)
★ YO, insert hook in **next** st, YO and pull up a loop, YO and draw through 2 loops on hook; repeat from ★ once **more**, YO and draw through all 3 loops on hook **(counts as one dc)**.

BACK POST DOUBLE CROCHET ***(abbreviated BPdc)***
YO, insert hook from **back** to **front** around post of st indicated ***(Fig. 4, page 2)***, YO and pull up a loop (3 loops on hook), (YO and draw through 2 loops on hook) twice.

BACK POST CLUSTER ***(abbreviated BP Cluster)*** (uses one st)
YO, insert hook from **back** to **front** and from **right** to **left** around post of next dc ***(Fig. 4, page 2)***, YO and pull up a loop, YO and draw through 2 loops on hook, YO, insert hook from **back** to **front** and from **left** to **right** around post of same st, YO and pull up a loop, YO and draw through 2 loops on hook, YO and draw through all 3 loops on hook. Skip st in front of BP Cluster.

AFGHAN

With Pink, ch 196 **loosely**.

Row 1 (Right side)**:** Dc in third ch from hook and in next 11 chs, 5 dc in next ch, dc in next 11 chs, ★ work double decrease, dc in next 11 chs, 5 dc in next ch, dc in next 11 chs; repeat from ★ across to last 2 chs, work ending decrease: 197 dc.

Note: Loop a short piece of yarn around any stitch to mark Row 1 as **right** side.

Row 2: Ch 2, turn; dc in next dc, (work BP Cluster, dc in next dc) 6 times, work BPdc around next dc, dc in same st, work BPdc around same dc, (dc in next dc, work BP Cluster) 6 times, ★ decrease, (work BP Cluster, dc in next dc) 6 times, work BPdc around next dc, dc in same st, work BPdc around same dc, (dc in next dc, work BP Cluster) 6 times; repeat from ★ across to last 2 dc, work ending decrease; finish off.

Row 3: With **right** side facing, join White with slip st in first dc; ch 3, (skip next 2 sts, sc in next st, ch 3) 4 times, skip next BPdc, (sc, ch 3) twice in next dc, skip next BPdc, sc in next dc, (ch 3, skip next 2 sts, sc in next st) 3 times, ch 1, ★ skip next 2 sts, dc in next dc, ch 1, (skip next 2 sts, sc in next st, ch 3) 4 times, skip next BPdc, (sc, ch 3) twice in next dc, skip next BPdc, sc in next dc, (ch 3, skip next 2 sts, sc in next st) 3 times, ch 1; repeat from ★ across to last 3 sts, skip next 2 sts, hdc in last dc to form last ch-3 sp: 77 sps.

Row 4: Ch 3, turn; (sc in next ch-3 sp, ch 3) 4 times, (sc, ch 3, sc) in next ch-3 sp, (ch 3, sc in next ch-3 sp) 4 times, ch 1, ★ skip next sc, dc in next dc, ch 1, (sc in next ch-3 sp, ch 3) 4 times, (sc, ch 3, sc) in next ch-3 sp, (ch 3, sc in next ch-3 sp) 4 times, ch 1; repeat from ★ across to last ch-3, hdc in center ch of last ch-3 to form last ch-3 sp.

Row 5: Ch 3, turn; (sc in next ch-3 sp, ch 3) 4 times, (sc, ch 3, sc) in next ch-3 sp, ★ (ch 3, sc in next ch-3 sp) 4 times, ch 1, skip next sc, dc in next dc, ch 1, (sc in next ch-3 sp, ch 3) 4 times, (sc, ch 3, sc) in next ch-3 sp; repeat from ★ across to last 5 ch-3 sps, (ch 3, sc in next ch-3 sp) across; finish off.

Row 6: With **right** side facing, join Pink with slip st in center ch of first ch-3; ch 2, 3 dc in each of next 4 ch-3 sps, 5 dc in next ch-3 sp, 3 dc in each of next 3 ch-3 sps, 2 dc in next ch-3 sp, ★ work double decrease, 2 dc in next ch-3 sp, 3 dc in each of next 3 ch-3 sps, 5 dc in next ch-3 sp, 3 dc in each of next 3 ch-3 sps, 2 dc in next ch-3 sp; repeat from ★ across to last ch-3, YO, insert hook in same sp, YO and pull up a loop, YO and draw through 2 loops on hook, YO, insert hook in center ch of last ch-3, YO and pull up a loop, YO and draw through 2 loops on hook, YO and draw through all 3 loops on hook: 197 sts.

Repeat Rows 2-6 until Afghan measures approximately $45^1/_2$" from beginning ch, ending by working Row 2.

8. DUCK

Shown on Front & Back Cover

Finished Size: $7\frac{1}{2}$" tall

MATERIALS

Worsted Weight Yarn:
- White - $1\frac{1}{2}$ ounces, (30 grams, 105 yards)
- Yellow - 15 yards
- Black - small amount

Crochet hook, size G (4.00 mm) **or** size needed for gauge
Polyester fiberfill
Yarn needle
1"w Ribbon - 23"

GAUGE SWATCH: 2" diameter
Work same as Head and Body through Rnd 3.

STITCH GUIDE

DECREASE
Pull up a loop in next 2 sts, YO and draw through all 3 loops on hook **(counts as one sc)**.

HEAD AND BODY

Rnd 1 (Right side)**:** With White, ch 2, 8 sc in second ch from hook; do **not** join, place marker.

Note: Markers are used to help distinguish the beginning of each round being worked. Place a 2" scrap piece of yarn before the first stitch of each round, moving marker after each round is complete.

Rnd 2: 2 Sc in each sc around: 16 sc.

Rnd 3: (Sc in next sc, 2 sc in next sc) around: 24 sc.

Rnd 4: (Sc in next 2 sc, 2 sc in next sc) around: 32 sc.

Rnd 5: (Sc in next 7 sc, 2 sc in next sc) around: 36 sc.

Rnds 6-13: Sc in each sc around.

Rnd 14: (Sc in next sc, decrease) around: 24 sc.

Stuff head firmly with polyester fiberfill.

Rnds 15-20: Sc in each sc around.

Rnd 21: (Sc in next sc, 2 sc in next sc) around: 36 sc.

Rnd 22: (Sc in next 5 sc, 2 sc in next sc) around: 42 sc.

Rnds 23-34: Sc in each sc around.

Rnd 35: (Sc in next sc, decrease) around: 28 sc.

Rnd 36: Decrease around: 14 sc.

Rnd 37: Sc in each sc around.

Stuff body firmly with polyester fiberfill.

Rnd 38: Decrease around: 7 sc.

Rnd 39: Skip next sc, (slip st in next sc, skip next sc) 3 times; slip st in next slip st, finish off.

BEAK

Rnd 1 (Right side)**:** With Yellow, ch 4 **loosely**; 2 sc in second ch from hook, sc in next ch, 4 sc in last ch; working in free loops of beginning ch ***(Fig. 3, page 2)***, sc in next ch, 2 sc in next ch; do **not** join, place marker: 10 sc.

Rnd 2: Sc in each sc around.

Rnd 3: (Sc in next sc, 2 sc in next sc) around: 15 sc.

Rnd 4: Sc in each sc around.

Rnd 5: Sc in next 5 sc, slip st in next sc, leave remaining 9 sc unworked; finish off leaving a long end for sewing.

FOOT (Make 2)

Row 1 (Right side)**:** With Yellow, ch 9 **loosely**; hdc in second ch from hook and in next ch, sc in next 5 chs, 4 sc in last ch; working in free loops of beginning ch, sc in next 5 chs, hdc in next 2 chs: 18 sts.

Row 2: Ch 2, turn; working in Back Loops Only ***(Fig. 1, page 2)***, hdc in first 2 hdc, sc in next 6 sc, 2 sc in each of next 2 sc, sc in next 6 sc, hdc in last 2 hdc, leave beginning ch unworked: 21 sts.

Row 3: Ch 2, turn; working in Back Loops Only, hdc in first 2 hdc, sc in next 7 sc, 2 sc in each of next 2 sc, sc in next 7 sc, hdc in last 2 hdc, leave turning ch unworked; finish off.

WING (Make 2)

Row 1: With White, ch 6 **loosely**; hdc in second ch from hook and in next ch, sc in next 2 chs, 4 sc in last ch; working in free loops of beginning ch, sc in next 2 chs, hdc in next 2 chs: 12 sts.

Row 2 (Right side)**:** Ch 2, turn; working in Back Loops Only, hdc in first 2 hdc, sc in next 3 sc, 2 sc in each of next 2 sc, sc in next 3 sc, hdc in last 2 hdc, leave beginning ch unworked: 15 sts.

Row 3: Ch 2, turn; working in Back Loops Only, hdc in first 2 hdc, sc in next 4 sc, 2 sc in each of next 2 sc, sc in next 4 sc, hdc in last 2 hdc, leave turning ch unworked: 17 sts.

Row 4: Ch 2, turn; working in Back Loops Only, hdc in first 2 hdc, sc in next 5 sc, 2 sc in each of next 2 sc, sc in next 5 sc, hdc in last 2 hdc, leave turning ch unworked; finish off.

ASSEMBLY

Using photo as a guide for placement:
- Stuff Beak lightly with polyester fiberfill and sew to Head between Rnds 9 and 13.
- With Black, add eyes using Satin Stitch ***(Fig. 5, page 2)***.
- Sew Wing to each side of Duck across Rnd 25.
- Sew Feet to bottom of Duck.
- Tie ribbon in a bow around neck.

Designed by Beth Ann Webber

Show us what you're working on!

Share your project photos with us on social media.
Tag us @leisureartsinc or use #leisurearts

Made in U.S.A.

Afghans designed by Tammy Kreimeyer.

We have made every effort to ensure that these instructions are accurate and complete. We cannot, however, be responsible for human error, typographical mistakes, or variations in individual work.

Items made and instructions tested by Janet Akins, Katie Galucki, Freda Gillham, Linda Graves, and Clare Stringer.